P9-CQF-952

Reed Hastings
and Netflix

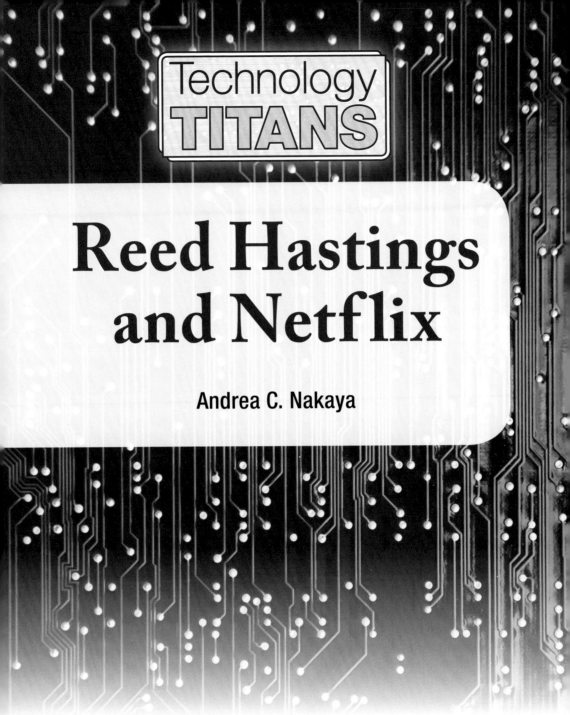

Technology TITANS

Reed Hastings and Netflix

Andrea C. Nakaya

ReferencePoint Press®

San Diego, CA

© 2016 ReferencePoint Press, Inc.
Printed in the United States

For more information, contact:
ReferencePoint Press, Inc.
PO Box 27779
San Diego, CA 92198
www.ReferencePointPress.com

LIBRARY OF CONGRESS CATALOGING-IN-PUBLICATION DATA

Nakaya, Andrea C., 1976-
  Reed Hastings and Netflix / by Andrea C. Nakaya.
     pages cm. -- (Technology titans)
  Includes bibliographical references and index.
  ISBN-13: 978-1-60152-878-0 (hardback)
  ISBN-10: 1-60152-878-7 (hardback)
  1. Netflix (Firm)--Juvenile literature. 2. Hastings, Reed, 1960---Juvenile literature. 3. Business-people--United States--Biography--Juvenile literature. 4. Video rental services--Juvenile literature. 5. Video recordings industry--Juvenile literature. 6. Internet videos--Juvenile literature. 7. Streaming technology (Telecommunications)--Juvenile literature. I. Title.
  HD9697.V544N4865 2016
  384.55'5092--dc23
  [B]
                                                                    2015003557

Contents

Changing How People Access Entertainment

In the first three decades of television history, viewers could only watch what was playing on their screens at the moment they turned them on. Shows and movies came on at regularly scheduled times each day and were broken up by advertising, which was how television networks made most of their money. In the earliest days, most viewers only had one or two television channels to watch, and only a few hours of shows were available each day.

As time passed, the number of television networks increased, and consumers had more content choices. By the 1990s cable and satellite services brought hundreds of channels to customers, and videocassette recorders (VCRs) allowed their owners to record programming to play back later. VCRs—and later digital video disc (DVD) players—also permitted consumers to rent movies from video stores and watch whenever they wanted. Yet despite these increasing options, for a long time entertainment was largely controlled by television (including cable) networks, which had complete control over entertainment content and schedules.

A New Way to Enjoy Entertainment

Although television networks are still dominant, today viewers have another option: they can stream their entertainment directly over the Internet. *Streaming* means that users receive a continuous flow of data from an online source and can watch content almost instantaneously on their own television or other digital device. The data is not saved on that device, as it is with downloading, but it is available at any time. Consumers who choose to stream their entertainment rather than watching it on television networks are no longer forced to adhere to a set entertainment schedule. Instead, they can watch whatever they want, at whatever time they choose to watch it.

Streaming is becoming increasingly popular. In 2014 the market research company Nielsen reported that about 2.6 million Americans were getting their information and entertainment content online rather than through cable or satellite television, more than double that of 2013. Numerous other studies confirm this trend. Many of these online customers are abandoning their cable and satellite subscriptions in favor of streaming; however, a growing number of young people have never used the traditional cable television model in the first place.

Computer science major and entrepreneur Reed Hastings has played a key role in the move to streaming. He predicted that it would become common well before it even became possible to stream movies and television shows. He created Netflix, a company that would be ready to capitalize on that trend and also help drive it. Although Netflix started out as a DVD-by-mail rental company, it quickly moved to streaming and has aggressively marketed its streaming service in the United States and numerous countries around the world. The company has become a major provider of streaming media on demand. Today it is estimated that Netflix accounts for more than 30 percent of all streaming traffic during peak hours in North America. Overall, concludes author John A. Byrne, "Hastings has changed how the entertainment business reaches its audience and how that audience is able to access content."[1]

"Hastings has changed how the entertainment business reaches its audience and how that audience is able to access content."[1]

—John A. Byrne, author.

Streaming Is Displacing Traditional Television

Hastings sees a future when the traditional television model will be gone completely, and people instead will subscribe to individual channels such as Netflix and access them online. He insists, "What's happening is all of entertainment is moving online. . . . Online is the future."[2] It is true that the number of online content providers continues to increase, and some major television channels, such as the popular network Home Box Office

(HBO), have recently announced that they will offer online service. The Netflix website insists that this is a trend that consumers will embrace. The company asserts, "People don't love the linear TV experience, where channels present programs at particular times on non-portable screens with complicated remote controls. Consumers have to navigate through a grid, or use DVRs which add an on-demand layer at the cost of storage and complexity. Finding good things to watch isn't easy or enjoyable." Overall, it says, "The linear TV channel model is ripe for replacement."[3]

Reed Hastings, pictured at a Netflix distribution plant in California, played a key role in the advent of movie and television streaming. Although Netflix began as a DVD-by-mail rental company, it is now a major provider of streaming media on demand.

In addition to encouraging increased streaming, Hastings has been an influential force in society's transition away from limiting the viewing experience to traditional television sets. As well as providing entertainment on demand, streaming allows consumers to enjoy content on any Internet-connected device. This includes compatible televisions but also cell phones, tablets, computers, and other electronic devices. According to a 2014 Harris poll of twenty-three hundred American adults, of those who regularly enjoy their entertainment via streaming, only 55 percent actually watch it on a television. "We now live in a world where every device is a television,"[4] explains media and technology analyst Richard Greenfield. As a result, many consumers no longer rely on actual televisions to enjoy entertainment. Instead, they utilize the large variety of other available devices. Technology writer Larry Magid talks about his entertainment consumption as an example:

> "The linear TV channel model is ripe for replacement."[3]
>
> —Netflix.

> Sometimes we watch . . . [shows] on our Internet-connected TV, but I also watch them on my laptop when traveling or when I want to sit in the backyard. I also watch shows on my iPad mini, my Kindle Fire HD and a variety of Android tablets. And even though watching video on a smartphone isn't an ideal experience, I've done it on iPhone and Android phones simply because it was convenient.[5]

Finding a Good Idea and Pursuing It

In numerous interviews Hastings has said that success comes from having a good, original idea and working hard to pursue it. In his case, such a philosophy has made him highly successful. His good idea was that streaming is the future of entertainment, and he has persevered with the goal of owning a company that provides streaming content to people around the world. Hastings's idea and his drive to make it a reality have not only led to a thriving business but also have helped change the entertainment industry entirely.

Chapter 1

Early Life

Wilmot Reed Hastings Jr. was born on October 8, 1960, in Belmont, Massachusetts, a suburb of Boston. His father was a lawyer. Hastings attended a private school called Buckingham Browne & Nichols in Cambridge, Massachusetts, which provides education from preschool through twelfth grade. At one time Hastings's father worked for the administration of President Richard Nixon, in which he served as an attorney for the Department of Health, Education, and Welfare. Hastings remembers that when he was about twelve years old his family was invited to Camp David one weekend by Elliot Richardson, who was a member of the president's cabinet. Camp David is a secluded country retreat located in Maryland, where the president often vacations. The Hastings family visited the retreat when the president was not there; however, the trip still created a lasting memory. Hastings recalls, "We rode around in golf carts, had a tour and I saw that President Nixon had a gold-colored toilet seat."[6]

Hastings graduated from high school in 1978. He took a year off before attending college, and during that time he worked as a door-to-door salesman, selling Rainbow brand vacuum cleaners. He says that his sales pitch was to clean the carpet with the customer's own vacuum cleaner, then to clean it with the Rainbow vacuum in order to show that the Rainbow was better. While the position started out simply as a summer job, Hastings stayed on past the summer. "I loved it, strange as that might sound," he says. "You get to meet a lot of different people."[7]

Studying Math at College

Following his year off, Reed attended Bowdoin College in Maine, where he studied math. When asked why he chose that major, he explained, "I majored in math because I found the abstractions beautiful and engaging."[8] During his time at Bowdoin he proved that, in addition to having an appreciation for the beauty of math, he was also a talented student. In 1981 he was awarded the Smyth Prize for receiving the highest grades in mathematics courses, and in 1983 he received the Hammond Prize for a graduating senior completing a major in mathematics with distinction. Bill Barker, one of his former professors at Bowdoin, remembers that in addition to his math skills, Hastings displayed the confidence and ingenuity that would later help him as an entrepreneur. "He has a desire to make things work right and get them going," Barker says. For example, Barker remembers that Hastings wrote a detailed plan of how the math department's calculus program should be revamped. He says, "We ran

As the son of a prominent lawyer, Hastings had a privileged childhood. When Hastings was about twelve, he and his family were invited to spend a weekend at Camp David (pictured), the secluded presidential retreat in Maryland.

the program for well over 10 years and no student had ever turned in anything like that. He was already in the mode of planning and doing things." He calls Hastings "a student you remember."[9]

While at Bowdoin, Hastings did not spend all his time doing math, however. He took on a role of leadership as the head of Bowdoin's Outing Club, a group that organizes various types of outdoor activities, such as hiking and canoeing. He also traveled overseas. During his junior year he spent a semester at the University of Bath in England. Hastings says, "I got to travel and hitchhike around Europe and North Africa and it definitely made me realize how little of the world I knew."[10]

A Love of Mathematics

In her book about Hastings and Netflix, journalist Gina Keating mentions that Hastings shares his love of mathematics with his maternal great-grandfather, Alfred Lee Loomis. Loomis used his knowledge of mathematics to make a lot of money. He worked as an investment banker on Wall Street, where, Keating says, "[He] applied a mathematical genius to investing."[11] That genius helped him make a lot of money. It also helped him avoid losing money when the stock market crashed in 1929. This crash, which ushered in the Great Depression, was the most devastating in US history, causing financial ruin for many people. Loomis was one of the few people who actually profited from the crash. In a book about Loomis, journalist Jennet Conant reports,

> He would later say that he had these mathematical charts that he used to follow industries, and that he saw that the bubble was going to burst. And very quietly in 1928, [Loomis and his company] . . . started pulling out of every stock that they had. They put it all in long-term government bonds and cash, and when Black Thursday came—October 24, 1929—they were sitting on a mountain of cash. And they did very, very well.[12]

Experience with the Marine Corps

Hastings graduated from college in 1983. He says that he was very interested in serving his country and initially planned to join the Marine

Corps after graduation. According to Hastings, he spent time with the Marines while he was still in high school: "[I] first joined the Marine Corps in their Platoon Leader Class, a sort of officers' candidate school. I spent summers in the Marines and between sopho-more and junior year I was in Quantico, Va., in boot camp." When Hastings actually experienced military discipline, however, he realized that he was not good at following orders in the way the Marines required, and he changed his mind. Members of the Marines are expected to follow orders without question, but Hastings explains that his personality led him to question the way everything was done. He says, "I found myself questioning how we packed our backpacks and how we made our beds. My questioning wasn't particularly encouraged, and I realized I might be better off in the Peace Corps."[13] As a result, Hastings says that he petitioned the recruiting office and subsequently left the Marines.

> "My questioning wasn't particularly encouraged [by the Marines], and I realized I might be better off in the Peace Corps."[13]
>
> —Reed Hastings.

Teaching in Africa

On his graduation day from college, Hastings left for training in the Peace Corps. The Peace Corps is a volunteer program that sends Americans to help people in other parts of the world. Peace Corps volunteers work to help improve economic and social conditions for communities in need. In addition, another major goal of the organization is to promote better understanding between the United States and other nations.

After Peace Corps training, Hastings was assigned to a high school in Swaziland in southern Africa, where he taught math. He says that he had eight hundred students and taught them geometry, algebra, and dif-ferential equations. Unlike the Marines, where individuals were required to follow orders, Hastings found that in Africa questions and innovation were important parts of life. He says, "There were no rules at all. Just use your initiative."[14]

In an interview, he describes what it was like living in Swaziland: "We were in a rural part of the country. We had no electricity and cooked with

The Benefits of Taking Risks

In a 2005 interview with *Inc.*, a business magazine and website, Hastings talks about the importance of taking risks and not always choosing what is safe and familiar. Although a risk means a chance of failure, he explains that there is also the chance of a significant reward. For example, Hastings took a risk when he joined the Peace Corps and traded the familiarity of the United States for Africa. While there was the risk that he could have been miserable there, in this case Hastings's risk paid off. He says, "It was an extremely satisfying experience." Taking a risk involves a lot of guesswork, but people can increase their chances of success by being smart about the risks they choose to take. For example, a person choosing to join the Peace Corps might research the values and goals of that organization in order to get a better idea if it will be a good fit. Hastings says, "Taking smart risks can be very gratifying. Guessing right is a skill developed over time. Not all smart risks work out, but many of them do."

Reed Hastings, as told to Patrick J. Sauer, "How I Did It: Reed Hastings, Netflix," *Inc.*, December 1, 2005. www.inc.com.

propane and wood. Corn was our staple. I lived in a thatch hut and slept on a cot." He also talks about how different the culture was. He says, "The high school graduation was really colorful. The celebrations were traditional and there were a lot of color wraps and furs. I was one of the few in Western dress."[15] Hastings stayed in Africa for approximately two and a half years, only going home for his sister's wedding. While he says that it was challenging to be away from home for so long, and that he missed many things about the United States, he also states that his time in Africa was a very satisfying experience.

The Need to Be Challenged

Although Hastings found teaching in Africa rewarding, he also felt that the pace of life there was too slow and that he was not being challenged enough. He remembers thinking, "I would never dribble away my days at home like this." Hastings says that his solution was to do something challenging. He explains, "The answer to my boredom and under-utilization was to get involved with the community as a whole instead of limiting myself to the school compound."[16] For example, he noticed that it was a struggle to transport water to the schoolhouse because it was at the top of a hill, so he helped to create a more efficient system. He also helped start a business harvesting honey from African bees. Writer Emma Peters explains the honey project in an article about Hastings: "For this project Hastings wrote a proposal requesting U.S. aid for Swazis to start their own safe and productive beekeeping businesses. The aid was granted, and Hastings, with the help of an agriculture teacher, taught an introductory course [about beekeeping.]"[17]

A beekeeper in the southern African country of Swaziland handles honeycomb. Hastings helped local people start their own beekeeping businesses while serving as a Peace Corps volunteer in Swaziland.

Hastings says that his time in Africa helped him as an entrepreneur. While there, he was forced to believe in his abilities and use his initiative to solve problems in challenging situations. He says that after the challenges he successfully faced in Africa, life's other challenges seemed much less daunting. He explains, "Once you have hitchhiked across Africa with ten bucks in your pocket, starting a business doesn't seem too intimidating."[18]

Graduate School

While in Africa, Hastings decided to return to the United States and attend graduate school. He says that he had to take a two-hour bus trip to Mbabane, the capital of Swaziland, to take the Graduate Record Examination, which is required for entrance to a US graduate school. He did not get into his first choice of school, the Massachusetts Institute of Technology in Cambridge, but he was accepted to Stanford University in California. In 1986 he began his master's degree in computer science there. "I really loved software," says Hastings about his interest in computer science. "I never loved anything so much."[19]

"Once you have hitchhiked across Africa with ten bucks in your pocket, starting a business doesn't seem too intimidating."[18]

—Reed Hastings.

Hastings initially found California very different from New England. He explains, "I had never been to California and arrived in late summer. Driving up to the campus I saw palm trees. It was dry and brown. I asked myself, 'Where's the ivy?'" However, he quickly grew to like his new environment. He says, "Within a week I had fallen in love with California."[20] According to one news story, Hastings told his parents, "You'll never see me again. . . . I've found nirvana."[21] He also fell in love with his studies. He recalls, "For the next couple of years I just programmed, and it was just such a joy I couldn't even imagine doing this as a job as opposed to a hobby. It was just such a joy to develop things."[22] Hastings received his degree—a master's degree in artificial intelligence—from Stanford University in 1988.

A Company of His Own

After graduation Hastings briefly worked for two other companies before going on to found one of his own. His first job was as a member of the

Family Background

Business journalist Gina Keating researched Hastings's background for a 2012 book about him, and she reports that he comes from a patrician—or wealthy and powerful—class of families. She says, "His mother's family were founding members of the *Social Register* [a directory that contains names and addresses of the social elite in the United States]; their births, marriages, and other life passages were chronicled in the *New York Times* society pages." According to Keating, Hastings's mother was presented to society in 1956. Making a formal debut into society is a tradition for the daughters of many upper-class families when they reach adulthood. Hastings's father, Wil Hastings, graduated from Harvard College in 1958.

Gina Keating, *Netflixed: The Epic Battle for America's Eyeballs.* New York: Penguin, 2012, p. 13.

technical staff at Schlumberger, a technology research lab in Palo Alto, California. Hastings's next job was as a software engineer, debugging software for a company called Coherent Thought. In 1991, at the age of thirty-one, he started his own business, which he named Pure Software. Pure Software created tools to help computer programmers debug their software programs. Its first debugging program was called Purify.

Pure Software was very successful and grew quickly. Hastings helped it expand by purchasing existing companies and merging with them. One of these merges resulted in the company changing its name to Pure Atria. In 1996 the company was doing so well that it went public, meaning that shares in the company would be publicly traded on the New York Stock Exchange. Although Pure Atria's rapid growth meant financial success, Hastings found it difficult to manage a company that was growing so quickly. He explains, "As the company grew from 10 to 40 to 120 to 320 to 640 employees, I found I was definitely underwater and over my head."[23] He says that while he had an excellent product, he did not feel that he had an excellent management style. Hastings says that he tried to fire himself twice, but he was unsuccessful. In addition to struggling to manage such a large company, he also disliked the company culture that had developed as a result of such rapid growth. He felt that the initial excitement he and his first employees experienced working at a new company had disappeared; for most employees, it had become just another job that lacked inspiration. In 2007 a journalist reported that Hastings felt that his company had gone "from being a heat-filled, everybody-wants-to-be-here place to a dronish, when-does-the-day-end sausage factory."[24]

Thinking About Business Culture

In 1997 Hastings received a way out of this unhappy situation when Pure Atria was purchased by a rival called Rational Software. Hastings reportedly received about $750 million, and he was left with both the freedom and the money to start another company and run it the way he wanted. Seeing Rational Software take over also gave him some insight into the type of company he wanted to lead. He says that when he saw how Rational Software worked, he realized that something better was possible. Hastings explains, "It was so different how they operated—the level of trust and the quality of interaction between them was impressive. . . . That gave me a North Star, something I wanted to grow toward."[25] He realized that he wanted his next company to be a place where he enjoyed coming to work, and where he worked with people he trusted and of whom he was proud.

> "As [my first company] grew from 10 to 40 to 120 to 320 to 640 employees, I found I was definitely underwater and over my head."[23]
>
> —Reed Hastings.

Just the Beginning

Hastings's first company had made him a millionaire, something that very few people are able to achieve in their lifetime. However, Pure Atria was just the beginning of Hastings's business career. He would go on to create a company that would become far bigger than his first. This new company would become important to the lives of millions of people in the United States and around the world.

Chapter 2

The Creation of Netflix

Reed Hastings has accomplished many things, but he is best known as the cofounder of Netflix. Netflix is a company that provides DVD rentals by mail in the United States and streaming video on demand in both the United States and numerous other countries around the world. Hastings and Marc Randolph—whom he had worked with at Pure Atria—founded the company in 1997. They created what has become one of the world's leading Internet television networks, available in almost fifty countries and with more than 53 million members worldwide.

The VCR

Although the idea of renting DVDs by mail or accessing movies and television shows online does not sound unique today, it was a new idea when Netflix was created. In 1997 DVD players were just starting to be sold in the United States, and they were very expensive—priced around $1,000. There was no such thing as streaming movies online because Internet service was far too slow. At most, a person with a good computer and fast Internet service might be able to stream a short video clip.

Instead, in 1997 a large number of people subscribed to cable television networks, which broadcast a large variety of entertainment content according to set schedules. In addition, a high percentage of Americans owned a VCR, the early tape-based, nondigital equivalent of the DVD player. Movies for the VCR came on video home system (VHS) videocassette tapes. VHS movies were relatively expensive to buy, so most consumers rented them at a video store instead. The majority of towns had numerous video rental stores, such as Blockbuster and Hollywood Video, which charged customers a rental fee that allowed them to keep the movie for one or two nights. Returning the movie after the deadline would incur late charges.

The Inspiration for Netflix

According to Hastings, these late charges are what inspired him to create Netflix. His story of how the company began has been repeated in numerous interviews and articles. Hastings says that he had rented the VHS movie *Apollo 13* and had forgotten to return it. He eventually realized that it was six weeks overdue, and he owed forty dollars in late fees. Hastings says that he was embarrassed and did not want to tell his wife about the fees. As a result of this experience, he started thinking about the movie rental business. One day on the way to the gym, Hastings says that he had the idea of creating a movie rental company that worked the same way as a gym membership. In the model he envisioned, rental customers

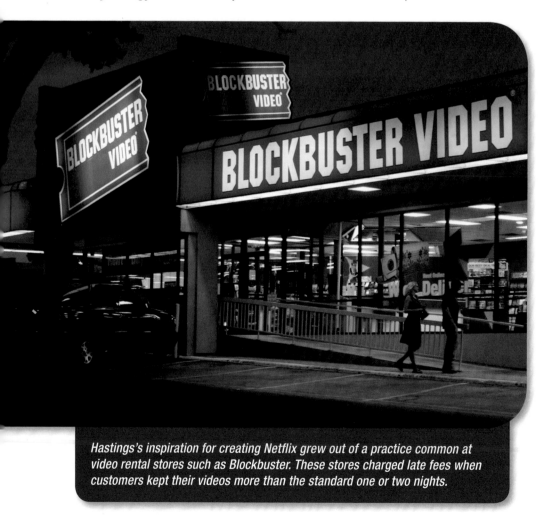

Hastings's inspiration for creating Netflix grew out of a practice common at video rental stores such as Blockbuster. These stores charged late fees when customers kept their videos more than the standard one or two nights.

would pay a monthly fee just like they did for the gym, and they could use the service as much or as little as they wanted. In addition, rather than renting movies at physical stores, customers would receive and return their movies by mail.

While Hastings thought that consumers would like the convenience of renting movies without having to go to a rental store, he realized that this model also posed a serious challenge. Unfortunately, it was very expensive to mail VHS tapes. He explains, "The problem is a VHS tape cost about four bucks to mail, four bucks to mail back, and four bucks to rent. There was a pretty small market for $12 video rental." However, he had the idea that DVDs would soon replace VHS tapes, and he realized that these were far cheaper to mail. He says that he and Randolph immediately tested the viability of his idea: "We bought a bunch of CDs [since DVDs were not yet widely available], ran down to the post office, and mailed them to ourselves. Then we had to wait a day to see if our great idea would work or would we get all these broken shards." Hastings and Randolph were happy to discover that there were no broken shards. Hastings says, "The next day the postman came and we opened them all up, and all the CDs were in perfect shape. And you could mail them for 36 cents then."[26] According to Hastings, this is the story of how Netflix was created.

> "We bought a bunch of CDs, ran down to the post office, and mailed them to ourselves."[26]
>
> —Reed Hastings.

Randolph's Version

Randolph tells a different story. He says that, in reality, the process of creating Netflix was far more complicated than Hastings simply being struck with inspiration on the way to the gym. Instead, Randolph says that coming up with Netflix involved a lot of thinking and discussion between the two men about what kind of business would make money. Of the *Apollo 13* story, he says, "These founding stories are just that— they're stories. They're constructs that we come up with to take what's a very messy process with input from many, many people, and condense it into a story which you can get across in a sentence or two." However,

The Netflix Mailer

While the design of Netflix's mailing packages might seem like a small detail, Hastings knew that it was important to the company's success. As a result, a lot of time was put into coming up with the best-possible design. The envelopes needed to be as small and lightweight as possible in order to reduce mailing costs; however, they also needed to protect the DVDs inside from breaking. In addition, Netflix wanted mailing envelopes that were both easy for customers to use and easy for Netflix employees to process. In its efforts to find the perfect mailers, Netflix has experimented with cardboard, plastic, and paper. It has even tried adding foam padding to protect the discs inside. In addition, it has tried both side-loading and top-loading envelopes to see which customers prefer. It finally settled on paper envelopes that load at the side.

Randolph says one part of Hastings's story is true: the part where they tested the viability of mailing DVDs. "We bought ourselves one of those little blue envelopes that you put the greeting cards in and we mailed a CD to Reed's house. We go up the steps to the Santa Cruz Post Office and dropped it in with a single first class stamp and by the next day when he came to pick me up he had the envelope in his hand. It had gotten to his house with the un-broken CD in it." As he remembers, "That was the moment where the two of us looked at each other and said, 'This idea just might work.'"[27]

A New Company

Regardless of how they came up with the idea, the fact is that Hastings and Randolph did create Netflix together. The two men had previously worked together at Pure Atria, where, according to Randolph, they often carpooled to work. Randolph had extensive marketing expertise and experience with starting new companies. His profile on the networking site LinkedIn states, "Prior to founding Netflix, Marc was a co-founder of more than half a dozen other successful start-ups in the e-commerce, media, enterprise software and portable device markets."[28]

The new company was incorporated on August 29, 1997. At that time Hastings and Randolph had not yet decided on a name for their company; however, they needed to put something on the incorporation documents. Randolph chose the name *Kibble, Inc.* He explains that the idea for this unusual name came from advice he had received from a mentor. The mentor advised him that rather than simply settling for a mediocre name, he should pick a name so bad that it would never become the company's permanent name. This means that the company would be forced to take the time to pick out a good name to replace the unusable one. In addition, says Randolph, he was advised to "pick something meaningful. It's a great way to start aligning everyone around what you think is really important." Randolph explains,

> So I called it Kibble. Kibble.com. Like the dog food. Unlaunchable name? You betcha! But ultimately I chose Kibble for a more important reason: It was to remind me (and everyone else at Netflix) never to forget that . . . "No matter how good the advertising, it's not a success if the dogs don't eat the dog food." In other words, you have to have both. Product and promotion. Steak and sizzle. Substance and spin.[29]

Hastings and Randolph were sure that their new company had that sizzle, and they soon came up with a name that they believed was a good fit. They replaced *Kibble* with *Netflix*, and the new company began operations in April 1998. Randolph was chief executive officer (CEO), and Hastings was chairman of the board of directors. In 1999 Hastings took over the role of CEO, and Randolph became executive producer of the Netflix website. Randolph only worked at Netflix for a relatively short time, leaving in 2002. He continued to serve on its board of directors until 2004. When Netflix started business in 1998, it had thirty employees and offered about nine hundred DVD titles for rent. Although nine hundred does not sound like a lot, DVDs were still relatively rare at that time, and this represented a large percentage of available DVD titles.

Finding the Right Company Model

Netflix was created as an alternative to the traditional rental-store model, but in the beginning it actually worked in a similar way. Netflix charged customers four dollars for a seven-day DVD rental and two dollars for shipping. The cost went down when additional DVDs were rented. Yet unlike traditional rental stores, Netflix had no physical stores for its customers to visit. Instead, customers selected their movies and paid for them online, and they received their movies and returned them via the mail. Netflix also offered DVDs for sale. Unfortunately, according to Hastings, this first model was not as successful as he had hoped. Quite simply, he says, "it wasn't working. People weren't coming back."[30]

It was not until 1999 that Netflix introduced its subscription plan. Under the new plan, customers paid a monthly fee of $15.95 and could rent as many movies as they wanted, four at a time. Customers set up an account on the Netflix website and created a queue of movies they wanted to watch. Each time they returned a movie, the next one on their queue would be mailed to them. If their first choice was not available, then they would receive the next available movie from their queue. In contrast to the first plan, this new model was very popular, and Netflix started to grow rapidly. By the end of 2000 it had more than 290,000 subscribers and was shipping hundreds of thousands of DVDs each week across the United States.

> "[The first Netflix business model] wasn't working. People weren't coming back."[30]
>
> —Reed Hastings.

Predicting the Future

With Netflix, Hastings has shown a remarkable ability to predict the future of entertainment and model his business in a way to capitalize on that future. He created a business based on DVD rentals and relying on Internet access at a time when very few Americans had either a DVD player or Internet access in their homes. In fact, when Netflix began less than 10 percent of American homes had a DVD player. And according to the US Census Bureau, in 1998 only 26 percent of US households had Internet access. Yet Hastings realized that soon both DVD players and Internet ac-

Netflix grew rapidly once it instituted a subscription plan. By the end of 2000 the company was shipping hundreds of thousands of DVDs each week to customers throughout the United States.

cess would become widespread, and his business was successful in part because he was ready to cater to this market as soon as it developed. "People thought this idea was crazy that consumers would rent [movies] through the mail," he remembers. "But it was precisely because it was a contrarian idea that enabled us to get ahead of our competitors."[31]

Randolph explains that when people did start buying DVD players, they often faced a challenge in finding a good selection of movies to watch. He says, "You could buy a DVD player, but good luck to you in trying to find a DVD to buy, no less to rent. And then if you go down to your corner store, you have a little selection of them, and they're all movies you don't want to watch."[32] Netflix worked hard to fill that need by offering a wide selection of movies. In addition to new releases, the company became known for offering obscure or older titles that were difficult to find anywhere else. In a 1998 interview Randolph explained, "We spend 90 percent of our time chasing down the last 5 percent of DVD titles."[33] He claimed that the company had the largest DVD inventory in the world.

Looking Ahead to Streaming

Even as he focused on the DVD market, Hastings says that he was looking even further ahead than a future where DVDs replaced VHS tapes. He believed that in the future people would not just use the Internet to access the Netflix website and pick a movie to be shipped to them. Instead, he believed they would actually watch their movies instantly via the Internet in a process called streaming. In one interview he insists, "That's why the company is called Netflix, not DVD-by-Mail."[34] *Fortune* writer Michael V. Copeland comments that this insight required Hastings to look well beyond what was possible at that time. He says, "Hastings' foresight is amazing, considering that back in 2000, less than 7% of U.S. homes had broadband."[35]

Changes in Entertainment

When Hastings began Netflix in 1997, only a small percentage of Americans had Internet access, and an even smaller number owned DVD players. Since Netflix relied on its customers having both, that percentage needed to increase in order for Netflix to become popular. As Hastings had predicted, this is exactly what happened. In 1997 it is estimated that close to 90 percent of American homes owned VCRs. However, that was the year that DVD players began to be sold to the public, and this new technology quickly caught up. By 2006—less than ten years later—Nielsen Media Research found that DVD players had surpassed VCRs in US homes. Internet access also spread quickly. According to the US Census Bureau, the percentage of households in the United States with Internet access increased from 26 percent in 1998 to 41 percent in 2000 and then to 50 percent in 2001.

Cinematch

In addition to predicting and catering to the rapidly growing market of DVD rentals, Hastings also helped Netflix become successful by creating a movie recommendation system for customers. While some people might think that such a system is a relatively minor detail for a movie rental company, it actually proved to be extremely popular with subscribers and greatly beneficial to Netflix. The system was called Cinematch.

It worked by having a Netflix customer rate movies with zero to five stars. Based on ratings and the customer's viewing history, Cinematch used computer algorithms to generate suggestions for other movies that the customer might enjoy. In a 2008 *New York Times* article, Hastings insisted that it would be too difficult and time consuming for Netflix subscribers to find movies they wanted to watch without Cinematch. He explains, "I

> "Hastings' foresight is amazing, considering that back in 2000, less than 7% of U.S. homes had broadband."[35]
>
> —Michael V. Copeland, a writer for *Fortune* magazine.

think that once you get beyond 1,000 choices, a recommendation system becomes critical. . . . People have limited cognitive time they want to spend on picking a movie."[36] Netflix customers seemed to agree because Cinematch caught on quickly. In a 2005 interview Hastings insisted that one reason Netflix's recommendations system was so popular was that it was very accurate: "We constantly invest in and improve our technology. Using all of our measurements, we know within a 10% range whether a movie will be a hit with a subscriber."[37]

In addition to helping customers find movies that they enjoyed, Cinematch helped the company. By steering customers toward older, less-known titles, Netflix helped manage supply and demand by reducing the number of people trying to rent the same few blockbuster movies at once. According to the *Times* article, 70 percent of Netflix rentals in 2008 were actually independent films or older movies; in comparison, 80 percent of rentals from traditional video stores were new blockbuster hits. In addition to reducing competition for new releases, Cinematch inspired people to watch more movies overall, which was also good for business.

The California State Board of Education

While Hastings was working hard to make Netflix successful, he was also pursuing something else that was very important to him: he wanted to help improve education in the United States. In 2000 he was appointed to the California State Board of Education by Governor Gray Davis. The board is in charge of making policies for elementary through high school education, including issues related to curriculum and academic standards. Hastings became president of the board in 2001. In 2004, however, he was forced out due to a disagreement over bilingual education policies. At that time some California students who did not speak English received instruction in their native language. Hastings thought they should also

First-grade students in Los Angeles work on their language skills. Hastings lost his seat on the California Board of Education after he called for some English-language instruction every day for students who did not speak English.

receive some instruction in English every day. According to Hastings, a group of Democratic legislators disagreed and forced him off the board. Overall he believes that he had a lot of support to continue as board president, but the politics tripped him up. He explains, "I lacked political deftness."[38] Yet leaving the board did not stop Hastings from actively trying to improve education. He continued to devote both time and money to this cause.

> "We constantly invest in and improve our technology."[37]
>
> —Reed Hastings.

A Difficult Beginning

Although Netflix eventually became successful, it had a difficult beginning. Despite its popularity, the company lost money for the first six years. In 2001, for instance, it had a net loss of $38.6 million. However, this does not mean that it was not successful. Hastings spent these years steadily gaining subscribers, increasing his inventory, and improving Netflix service. Netflix soon had hundreds of thousands of customers across the United States. It was not long before it would make a profit as well.

Chapter 3

Success at Netflix

In 2010 Jeffrey L. Bewkes, the chief executive of the major media company Time Warner, publicly dismissed Netflix as a serious contender in the entertainment business by comparing it to the small country of Albania. "It's a little bit like, is the Albanian army going to take over the world?," he said. "I don't think so."[39] Yet despite starting out small, Hastings did in fact plan to take over the world of entertainment on demand. He says that comments like this simply increased his drive to do so. Regarding Bewkes's statement, he says, "For the next year, I wore Albanian Army dog tags around my neck. It was my rosary beads of motivation."[40]

Bewkes is not the only critic who has underestimated the position that Netflix would reach in the entertainment industry. In 2005 stock analyst Michael Pachter also dismissed Netflix with a comment that became famous because of how wrong it turned out to be. Pachter called the company "a worthless piece of crap with really nice people running it."[41] In spite of the stream of critical comments, Netflix proved to be popular with consumers. After its creation in 1997 the company steadily gained subscribers, earned growing revenue (despite running at a loss), and increased substantially in worth.

> "[Netflix is] a worthless piece of crap with really nice people running it."[41]
>
> —Michael Pachter, stock analyst.

Going Public

Netflix's first major step toward becoming profitable was to become a public company, which it did in May 2002. When a company goes public, it sells shares on the stock market. People who buy the shares become part owners in that company. The company benefits by earning money from the sale of these shares. When it went public in 2002, Netflix sold

5.5 million shares, earning $82.5 million dollars. This money would allow it to pay off some of its debts and expand further.

Going public also meant that Netflix was now accountable to all the new part owners in the company. For instance, it had to issue regular public reports about the state of the company and its finances. However, Hastings was happy about this new level of responsibility. He insists, "I find running a public company to be a lot more fun and exciting [than a private one]. What you do matters more to the world, there are more stakeholders, and management performance is more visible."[42]

Reed Hastings had reason to smile when this photograph was taken in 2002, the year his company went public. Through the sale of shares, the company earned enough to pay off debts and expand.

In 2003, the year after it went public, Netflix finally made a profit. Hastings remembers when the company hit a million subscribers that year. He says, "I was down in Arizona in 2003 visiting one of our distribution centers on the outskirts of Phoenix. It was raining, and my umbrella wasn't working, so I walked the half mile from the distribution center to the hotel." He remembers, "I got the message on my BlackBerry that we hit a million [subscribers] that day while I was walking in the rain. It was this beautiful moment where I was just so elated that we were going to make it, and that was also the first quarter that we turned profitable. It was a magic walk."[43] In its 2003 annual report, Netflix stated that net income for the year was $6.5 million, compared with a net loss of $20.9 million in 2002.

Competitors

Unfortunately, Hastings's success quickly spurred competitors. He believes that the decision to go public was also a major reason for the sudden onslaught of competitors. When Netflix starting making public

The First Attempt to Go Public

The year 2002 was not the first time Netflix tried to become a public company. Its first attempt was in 2000, but it withdrew after it failed to attract enough interest. That year the stock market was experiencing something many people refer to as the burst of the dot-com bubble. Prior to 2000 there had been an explosion of dot-com companies—companies that existed mainly on the Internet. Investor interest in these companies led to their being worth more and more on the stock market, which is what is meant by the term *bubble*. Although many of these companies were worth a lot on the stock market, in reality they were not making a profit. When investors started to realize that investing in these companies might be unwise, prices dropped and the bubble burst. As a result, many investors were wary of Internet companies such as Netflix, and Hastings was not able to attract enough interest to go public in 2000.

financial reports, its competitors were able to see just how successful a DVD-by-mail company could be. In Hastings's opinion, "what triggered Amazon and Blockbuster to compete with us is they could see how profitable we were and how fast we were growing."[44] According to a 2005 *New York Times* story, Hastings wished that he had postponed going public in order to delay that competition.

After Netflix went public, its two biggest competitors became Walmart and Blockbuster. In 2003 Walmart began its own DVD-by-mail service. Netflix was charging $19.95 a month for unlimited DVDs, which customers could receive three at a time. Walmart introduced the same plan but priced it at $18.86. In 2004 Blockbuster started Blockbuster Online, another DVD-by-mail service, pricing it at $19.99. *New York Times* writer David Pogue commented at the time, "All three services look and work almost exactly alike. Netflix must be furious."[45] A price war followed in which Netflix reduced its subscription price to $17.99, Blockbuster reduced its plan to $17.49, and Wal-Mart dropped the price to $17.36. Then Blockbuster lowered its price again, to $14.99. Netflix reacted by promoting a new plan, with two DVDs at a time for $14.99.

> "What triggered Amazon and Blockbuster to compete with us is they could see how profitable we were and how fast we were growing."[44]
>
> —Reed Hastings.

Ultimately, despite reducing their prices, neither Walmart nor Blockbuster was able to successfully compete with Netflix. In 2005 Walmart dropped out of the competition after making a deal with Netflix: Walmart would encourage its subscribers to join Netflix for DVD rentals, and Netflix would encourage its customers to go to Walmart if they wanted to buy DVDs. However, this deal also led to a lawsuit against both companies—initiated by a group of Netflix subscribers—that alleged the companies had worked together so that Walmart could take over the DVD sales market and Netflix could take over the rental market. Walmart agreed to a settlement, but Netflix eventually won the lawsuit in 2011.

Netflix Dominates

The rivalry with Blockbuster lasted far longer than with Walmart; however, Netflix was ultimately the winner in that competition too. Ironically, before running Blockbuster out of business, Netflix actually had offered to partner with the company. In 2000, when Netflix was still losing money and was a much smaller company than Blockbuster, Hastings had met with Blockbuster CEO John Antioco and had proposed a partnership between the two companies. Barry McCarthy, Netflix's former chief financial officer, remembers going to the meeting with Hastings and Randolph. He says, "Reed had the chutzpah to propose to them that we run their brand online and that they run [our] brand in the stores and they just about laughed us out of their office."[46] When Blockbuster declined the partnership, that decision marked the beginning of a losing battle with Netflix. Blockbuster invested millions of dollars and tried a number of strategies—such as abolishing late fees—in an effort to beat its competitor. Nonetheless, it was unsuccessful and filed for bankruptcy in 2010. Many people believe that one of the reasons Blockbuster failed was that it had physical rental stores in addition to its online business. This means that the cost of running its business was higher than that of Netflix, which existed exclusively online.

> "Netflix's business is anything but simple, and that's why the competition has faltered."[47]
>
> —Rick Newman, journalist and author.

Journalist Rick Newman comments that numerous competitors have tried unsuccessfully to duplicate Netflix's success without realizing that achieving such success is not as easy as it looks. He says, "As Netflix became successful, competitors emerged because its business model seemed simple: Simply keep DVDs in a warehouse and mail them out when orders came in. But Netflix's business is anything but simple, and that's why the competition has faltered."[47] Netflix has been able to provide a unique combination of innovation, excellent customer service, and forward thinking that has made it successful when many other companies have failed.

The Importance of Customer Service

Some people believe that Netflix's focus on excellent customer service is a key reason why it has triumphed over its competition. Stanford Business School professor and entrepreneur Andy Rachleff says, "Most

A Netflix employee removes returned DVDs from their mailing envelopes. The company prides itself on providing excellent customer service.

people think you should be riveted on the competition." However, he insists that this is not actually the way to success. He says, "Absolutely not. Be riveted on delighting your customer. If you do that all they can do is follow you. That's why Netflix is so far ahead of Blockbuster. They're focused on delighting the customer."[48] Journalist James Ledbetter agrees. He points out that by creating good relationships with its subscribers, Netflix has created a huge following: "Netflix . . . has built its relationship with customers extremely carefully and successfully—some 15 million people now send Netflix money every month. (How many nonutility companies can boast that?)"[49]

Hastings has often spoken about how this passion for pleasing his customers motivates him more than anything else. He explains that by focusing on his customers, they feel strongly about staying with Netflix: "Netflix has customer loyalty; it's a passion brand."[50] Randolph agrees that the heart of Netflix has always been about helping people find movies they will enjoy. He says, "We very, very early came up with the idea that Netflix would be about finding movies you love."[51]

In addition to focusing on the big picture of helping people find movies they love, Netflix does not neglect the smaller details of customer service. In 2005 journalist Pogue compared the competition between Netflix, Blockbuster, and Walmart and concluded that Netflix easily surpassed the other two companies in customer service. He says, "Netflix's act is decidedly together; its customer service stories sometimes verge on the heroic." He gives an example of how Netflix went out of its way to help one of its customers: "'I once somehow managed to mail back one of my

An Easy Target for Thieves

Netflix is well known for its red DVD-mailing envelopes. They have become a symbol of the company. However, because the envelopes are so easy to identify, they are also an easy target for thieves. Numerous people have been caught stealing Netflix DVDs from the mail, including a number of postal workers. In one extreme case, Myles Weathers, a postal employee in Massachusetts, was caught stealing Netflix movies from the postage facility where he worked. According to news reports, Weathers was arrested in 2008 after he was filmed taking DVDs and putting them into his backpack. Officials had been investigating the DVD thefts after it was discovered that a suspiciously high number had occurred at that particular post office. Weathers reportedly admitted to stealing more than three thousand DVDs.

own DVD's in a Netflix return envelope,' one reader wrote to me. 'I was certain that I would never see that disc again, but I sent an e-mail to customer service anyway. I got a prompt reply saying that they would locate my DVD and send it back to me—and they did. No charge.'"[52]

Throttling

Striving for excellent customer service has not stopped Netflix from receiving some criticism though. One Netflix practice that has generated criticism is the way Netflix treats its heavy renters differently than new subscribers or infrequent renters. Subscribers who rent a large number of movies every month sometimes have their shipments slowed down, and they are often put at the back of the line for new releases and popular DVDs, which are given instead to infrequent renters and new subscribers first. For example, in a 2006 news story Netflix customer Manuel Villanueva claimed that he initially received about eighteen to twenty-two DVDs per month until the Netflix system slowed him down to only about thirteen a month. Some people have named this practice *throttling*.

In 2004 a group of customers sued Netflix over this practice, but the lawsuit did not change Netflix's policies. The company settled the case. In addition, it revised its terms of service so that it could continue its practices without being subject to another lawsuit. Its "DVD Terms and Conditions" now state, "In determining priority for shipping and inventory allocation, we may utilize many different factors, including the number and type of DVDs you rent through our service, the membership plan you select, as well as other uses of our service by you. For example, if all other factors are the same, we give priority to those members who receive the fewest DVDs through our service."[53] In response to continuing criticism, Hastings has strongly defended Netflix's allocation policies, insisting that the majority of customers are extremely happy with their Netflix service.

The Contest to Improve Cinematch

To provide even better customer service, in 2006 Netflix announced a competition to improve Cinematch, its movie recommendation system.

It would give $1 million to whoever could make Cinematch's predictions at least 10 percent more accurate. Thousands of people from countries all over the world worked hard in an attempt to claim the prize, and the competition lasted almost three years. "It's been quite a drama," said Neil Hunt, Netflix's chief product officer, describing the contest's progress. "At first, a whole lot of teams got in—and they got 6-percent improvement, 7-percent improvement, 8-percent improvement, and then it started slowing down, and we got into year two. There was this long period where they were barely making progress, and we were thinking, 'maybe this will never be won.'"[54] A team called BellKor's Pragmatic Chaos, led by AT&T Research engineers, finally was announced as the winner in 2009. However, the contest was not as successful as Netflix had hoped. That same year a lawsuit was brought against the company, arguing that it had violated subscriber privacy by releasing user data to competitors in the contest. Netflix settled the suit and canceled the planned second contest.

Distribution

As the number of Netflix subscribers grew, the company also tried to improve its service by adding distribution centers. This would allow it to process rentals more quickly. Its first distribution center was in the San Francisco Bay Area, and subscribers who lived far away from that center might have to wait days to receive their DVDs. "It wasn't a very consumer-satisfying experience, except in the San Francisco Bay Area,"[55] says Hastings. In 2002 Netflix announced that it would open ten additional centers around the country, with the goal of customers receiving movies in only one or two days like many on the West Coast did. By 2005 Netflix had thirty distribution centers, and by 2011 there were fifty-eight. The expansion of distribution centers meant that most customers now received their DVDs in only a day or two.

Streaming

In 2007 Netflix further increased the value of a Netflix membership by adding a streaming feature to its website. In a "Watch Now" section, subscribers could choose to stream a movie instantly rather than waiting

Hastings was concerned about wait times for customers who lived far from the original San Francisco Bay Area Netflix distribution center. To fix this problem the company opened additional centers around the country.

to receive it in the mail. They did not have to pay extra for this feature, although they were only allowed a certain number of hours of streaming, depending on what type of plan they had. For example, under the most expensive plan of $17.99, they could stream eighteen hours each month. About one thousand titles were initially available to stream.

Providing streaming meant that Netflix had to make some significant changes to the way it did business. Firstly, it faced different requirements in order to obtain streaming content because streaming rules differ from DVD rental rules. Under DVD rental rules, Netflix can simply buy a DVD, then rent it out as often as needed. Yet to stream movies, Netflix must enter a licensing agreement with the studio that owns the movie. If that agreement ends, then Netflix no longer has permission to stream that content. When Netflix first started streaming, televisions could not connect to the Internet. Thus, Netflix also had to make agreements with companies such as Roku, which created television-streaming equipment.

Despite the challenges of obtaining movies and television shows for streaming, Netflix soon managed to provide a wide variety of content. One of its biggest licensing agreements was in 2008 with Starz, a premium cable television company. The Starz deal allowed Netflix subscribers to stream an additional twenty-five hundred titles. Because Hastings believed so strongly that in the future everyone would stream their movies and television shows rather than rent DVDs, he worked hard to expand his streaming service. In 2011 he explained, "We want to focus on a simple proposition: unlimited streaming for $7.99 per month. Our big focus is taking that simple proposition around the globe."[56]

A Very Successful Company

By 2010 Netflix had proven its critics wrong and was a highly successful company. That year *Fortune* named Hastings Businessperson of the Year. The magazine explains that achieving this title was not an easy feat:

> Reed Hastings isn't supposed to be here—not on a list of the year's top businesspeople, and certainly not on the cover of

Fortune. His DVD-by-mail company, Netflix, was supposed to have flamed out by now, a one-trick pony that was destined to be crushed by Blockbuster or Wal-Mart or Apple or you name it. . . . Whoops. Not only has Hastings earned the No. 1 spot on Fortune's Businessperson of the Year list, he and Netflix are also killing it.[57]

By 2011 Netflix company shares—a measure of the company's public worth—were at $304.79, the highest they had ever been. The company also announced that it had passed the 20 million subscriber mark. In a January 2011 letter to shareholders, it announced, "We are thrilled to be able to report another outstanding quarter. . . . Our huge subscriber growth, fueled by the excitement of watching instantly, impressed even us."[58] However, Hastings was about to send Netflix prices plummeting drastically and subscribers fleeing by making a decision that he would quickly come to regret.

> "Not only has Hastings earned the No. 1 spot on Fortune's Businessperson of the Year list, he and Netflix are also killing it."[57]
>
> —*Fortune* magazine.

Chapter 4

Persevering to Reach His Goals

By 2011 Hastings had helped make Netflix a successful company, and many people were confident that its success would continue. Market-Watch, a website of publishing and financial information firm Dow Jones, reports that the company's net income for 2010 was $160.85 million. Unfortunately, 2011 turned out to be a tumultuous year for the company. Hastings made some decisions that cost it a lot of customers and caused its value to plummet drastically. Yet this was not the end of Netflix. Just as Hastings had put his hard work and ingenuity into creating Netflix and reaching a high level of success in 2011, he persevered again to help the company rebound. Despite losing hundreds and thousands of subscribers and the confidence of many in the business world, with Hastings's help Netflix again rose to a position of dominance in the entertainment industry.

A Price Increase

The decisions that almost destroyed Netflix were significant changes to its pricing and subscription plans, which it announced in the latter part of 2011. Hastings strongly believed that streaming, not DVD rentals, would be the technology of the future. As a result, he felt that Netflix needed to be aggressive about moving quickly to dominate the streaming market or it would be eclipsed by other companies. He explained, "Companies rarely die from moving too fast, and they frequently die from moving too slowly."[59] In order to help the company focus on streaming, Hastings decided to split up its DVD-by-mail and streaming services and also to increase subscription prices.

The price increase came first. Until this point subscribers had been able to receive both DVDs by mail and streaming service for only $9.99 a month. Netflix announced that customers would now have to pay $7.99 for unlimited one-at-a-time DVD rentals or $11.99 for two-at-a-time rentals. Unlimited streaming would be available for $7.99. This meant that customers who wanted both DVD rentals and streaming would now have to pay $15.98 instead of only $9.99. The price change amounted to an increase of approximately 60 percent for customers who wanted to continue with both services. In a *Netflix* blog post detailing the increase, marketing officer Jessie Becker insisted, "We think $7.99 is a terrific value for our unlimited streaming plan and $7.99 a terrific value for our unlimited DVD plan."[60]

> "Companies rarely die from moving too fast, and they frequently die from moving too slowly."[59]
>
> —Reed Hastings.

Customers, however, did not think it was so terrific. A large number immediately expressed anger and unhappiness with the change and said they planned to cancel their subscriptions. For instance, one customer commented on the *Netflix* blog, "No additional benefit, 60% increase. And not even a discount for ordering the DVDs and streaming—we'll be dropping."[61] Another said, "I know I'll be cancelling my service and going with Blockbuster soon."[62] Yet another commented, "Boo! You're raising my price by 33% and giving me nothing more. I won't pay it."[63]

Qwikster

In response to the large number of negative customer reactions, Hastings apologized for the abrupt nature of the change, saying, "I messed up. I owe everyone an explanation." However, he stuck to his new plan, explaining that he believed DVD rentals and streaming had different requirements and should be separated. Further, he announced, the company would actually split up its streaming and DVD-by-mail service into two separate companies. He said that he was creating a new company called Qwikster to oversee the DVD-by-mail service. Netflix would oversee streaming. If a customer wanted both DVD-by-mail and streaming, they would now have to use two separate websites and would receive

A Netflix customer demonstrates the company's online movie service. Hastings strongly believed that streaming would be the technology of the future, and he wanted his company to aggressively pursue this market.

two separate bills. Hastings defended the decision, stating, "Some members will likely feel that we shouldn't split the businesses, and that we shouldn't rename our DVD by mail service. Our view is with this split of the businesses, we will be better at streaming, and we will be better at DVD by mail."[64]

Trouble for Netflix

Hastings vastly underestimated the depth of customer unhappiness. In just a few months Netflix lost eight hundred thousand subscribers. In a

Facebook posting, Hastings commented on just how angry Netflix investors were, joking that someone might try to poison him. "In Wyoming with 10 investors at a ranch/retreat," he posted. "I think I might need a food taster. I can hardly blame them."[65] As a result of the overwhelmingly negative response to his plan and the massive loss of subscribers, in October 2011 he announced that he would no longer be pursuing Qwikster or the plan to split up the DVD-by-mail and streaming services.

Hastings's ability to recognize his mistake and apologize was appreciated by many people; however, the fact remained that Netflix was now in trouble. Katherine Milkman, a business professor at the University of Pennsylvania's Wharton School, argues that while Hastings made a bad decision with Qwikster, he was at least mature enough to recognize that mistake and try to fix it. In contrast, she says, in too many cases "people want to save face and don't think, what's best for my company at this point?"[66] Yet although he may have placated some people by publicly recognizing his mistake, Hastings still had a lot of financial damage to undo. In addition to losing thousands of subscribers, the company experienced a huge drop in stock prices. Hastings also received a significant pay cut.

> "People want to save face and don't think, what's best for my company at this point?"[66]
>
> —Katherine Milkman, a business professor at the University of Pennsylvania's Wharton School.

The Path Back to Success

Hastings gave up on the Qwikster plan, but he did not give up on Netflix. He worked hard to get its subscribers back, and in less than a year he had turned the company's brief failure around, setting it on the path to becoming even more successful than before. MarketWatch reports that net income for 2012 dropped to only $17.15 million; however, by the end of 2013 it was back up to $112.4 million. Looking back at the problems caused by the Qwikster decision, Hastings sees it as a minor dip in Netflix's otherwise very successful history. In a 2012 interview for *Vanity Fair*, Hastings stressed that the problems Netflix faced in 2011 were so minor that they did not cause him a lot of stress. In fact, he says, "when we had our stumble . . . I slept well every night."[67] He insists that the real issue is that Netflix was trying to be one of the first companies to make the transition from DVDs to providing streaming content. He points out that despite temporarily suffering after its Qwikster decision, Netflix has managed to become very successful as a streaming pioneer: "Most businesses, like Kodak [a company that is best known for photographic film products] or Blockbuster, go out of business when confronted with a radical new business model. And the fact that we didn't, and were able to make the shift from DVDs to streaming, is the bigger story."[68]

A Unique Company Policy

Many people believe that in addition to Hastings's vision of the future, Netflix's success is due to the unique way that he runs his company. Hastings explains that he does not tolerate employees who can simply do their job adequately; instead, he focuses on having a team of employees who excel at their jobs. Patty McCord, chief talent officer at Netflix from 1998 to 2012, says that people who do not display this high level of performance do not stay at Netflix for long. She explains how the Netflix hiring policy evolved: "[We realized] if we wanted only 'A' players on our team, we had to be willing to let go of people whose skills no longer fit, no matter how valuable their contributions had once been. Out of fairness to such people—and, frankly, to help us overcome our discomfort with discharging them—we learned to offer rich severance packages."[69] While it is unlikely that Netflix would be so successful today without Hastings, his team of talented employees also deserves credit for the company's achievements. Hastings explains that he relies heavily on his team. He says, "I take pride in making as few decisions as possible, as opposed to making as many as possible."[70]

> "[We realized] if we wanted only 'A' players on our team, we had to be willing to let go of people whose skills no longer fit, no matter how valuable their contributions had once been."[69]
>
> —Patty McCord, chief talent officer at Netflix from 1998 to 2012.

Most employees have positive things to say about the experience of working at Netflix. For example, software developer Siddharth Anand describes his experience and echoes Hastings's statement that employees play an important role in the success of the company: "We have to be leaders. In general, the responsibility of each employee is to move the company

Ridiculing Qwikster

When Hastings announced Qwikster, he included a video of himself and Andy Rendich, who would be the CEO of the new company. However, the video was poorly made and quickly resulted in widespread ridicule. *Vanity Fair* writer William D. Cohan describes the video:

> Accompanying this surprising announcement [of Qwikster] was a lame video of Hastings along with Andy Rendich. . . . Hastings was rocking the casual look in a Gap T-shirt underneath some sort of flimsy, ill-fitting teal work shirt. His Oakley sunglasses rested in front of him on his IBM ThinkPad. At one point, he flubbed a line and repeated it—a homey touch that remained in the video. He observed correctly on the Netflix Blog, "You'll probably say we should avoid going into moviemaking after watching it."

The video quickly resulted in parodies by various comedians, including the popular comedy sketch show *Saturday Night Live* and the late-night Conan O'Brien show.

William D. Cohan, "Seeing Red," *Vanity Fair*, February 2, 2012. www.vanityfair.com.

in a positive direction. The feeling of playing a critical role permeates the environment." He insists, "It has been the best place I have ever worked."[71] Walter Stokes, who worked at Netflix as the director of information technology operations, says that he liked the fact that at Netflix he worked with highly capable colleagues. "Everyone is smarter than you," he says, "There's no deadwood here. If the wrong person is in the job, the emphasis is on doing what you have to do to get the right person."[72]

Freedom and Responsibility

In addition to looking for employees who excel at their jobs, Netflix strives to find employees who will act responsibly, always keeping the

NETFLIX

OUR GOAL!!!

TO ALWAYS
DELIVER THE
CORRECT PLAYABLE
DISC THE NEXT DAY
AT A COST
UNATTAINABLE BY
OUR
COMPETITORS!

netflix.com

A sign reminds Netflix employees to carefully inspect all incoming and outgoing items. The company says it relies on employees to make good decisions based more on common sense than on rules.

company's best interests in mind. Unlike the majority of other companies, where human resources departments create collections of rules and policies about what employees can and cannot do, Netflix relies on its employees to use their own logic and common sense to make good decisions. McCord insists that the usual human resources rules are not necessary at Netflix. She explains, "If you're careful to hire people who will put the company's interests first, who understand and support the desire for a high-performance workplace, 97% of your employees will do the right thing."[73] At Netflix the other 3 percent—those people who are not able to do the right thing—are given a severance package. Those who do display the desired level of responsibly are given a large amount of freedom. For example, there is no limit to how many vacation days Netflix employees can take as long as they do their jobs well.

Hastings exemplifies this idea of freedom. He reportedly does not even have his own office. Instead, according to one news story, "he roams around the company, pitching in where needed."[74] The reporter says that when Hastings does need some privacy, he goes up to the company's glass conference room, which has a spectacular view of the Santa Cruz Mountains.

A Passion for Education

While Hastings's career has been mainly focused on Netflix, he has also put a substantial amount of energy into the field of education, a subject about which he is passionate. His interest in education dates back to his time as a Peace Corps teacher in Africa. According to Hastings, once he had gained financial means, he wanted to try and make a real difference in education. "After Pure Software, I had a bunch of money, and I didn't really want to buy yachts and such things." Instead, he says, "I wanted to find something important to do. And I started looking at education, trying to figure out why our education is lagging when our technology is increasing at great rates and there's great innovation in so many other areas—health care, biotech, information technology, movie-making. Why not education?"[75] Before starting Netflix, Hastings even briefly returned to Stanford University to study for a master's degree in education. Although he did not finish the degree, he has actively pursued his goal of trying to improve the field of education. Michael Kirst, a professor of education, applauds the amount of effort Hastings has put into educational reform. He comments, "So many people in business get interested in education or criticize education, but very few are like Reed, who said, 'I've got to spend some time and study the field in depth.'"[76]

Expanding Charter Schools

One of Hastings's main focuses has been on charter schools. Like public schools, charter schools are free to students. However, charter schools operate independently from the public school system. Charter schools have more freedom to be innovative in the way they teach students, and they are usually held more accountable than public schools to perform to high standards. Therefore, some people think that charter school education is more effective than public schooling. Hastings agrees. He explains that when education is controlled by one entity—the government—there is little incentive for innovation. Yet because charter schools provide

Removing the "Friends" Feature

When Netflix eliminated the "Friends" feature on its website, the change provoked angry customer reactions. The feature had been added in 2004 and allowed subscribers to connect with friends' accounts in order to see what they were watching and what they thought of particular movies. With Friends, Netflix customers could share ratings, comments, and suggestions about movies with their friends. Many subscribers were angry when Netflix deleted the feature, but the company insisted that less than 2 percent of Netflix subscribers actually used Friends. In comparison, it argued that about 50 percent were streaming content, so it had decided to focus on improving that part of its service instead. A Netflix post stated, "No company has unlimited resources and we decided to move engineering development time and resources from a little used feature to support and maintain the things that benefit all Netflix members as the service evolves—more devices for streaming and better encoding, for example."

Todd Yellin, "Friends Update," *Netflix* (blog), March 17, 2010. http://blog.netflix.com.

competition, he believes this leads to innovation. He insists, "We're finding out more and more that competitive forces can provide great improvement in services." When there are multiple groups trying to provide a service, he explains, "they all compete for impact and prestige and donor dollars. And they have different approaches to the problems and that's healthy."[77]

Hastings has worked to help charter schools expand. For example, in 1998 he was part of a campaign that successfully forced California to change restrictive charter school law in order to make it easier to start a charter school. He has also donated millions of dollars to help develop high-quality charter schools. For instance, he helped start Aspire Public Schools, a network of thirty-seven charter schools in California and Tennessee. Hastings's friend Nick McKeown, an associate professor of electrical engineering and computer science, comments on Hastings's dedication to education: "He is absolutely driven to improve the level of education in this country."[78]

> "[Hastings] is absolutely driven to improve the level of education in this country."[78]
>
> —Nick McKeown, an associate professor of electrical engineering and computer science.

Improving Education with Technology

In addition to improving education through charter schools, Hastings is focused on using technology to improve learning. He believes the use of software programs in schools can provide more flexibility to teachers and students. For instance, within one classroom a teacher can use a math program that allows one third-grade student to work on grade-level math while a more advanced third-grader can study fifth-grade math. However, although he is in favor of technology in education, Hastings also stresses that some types of teaching cannot currently be done by computer. Whereas software programs may be good for teaching subjects that have definite correct answers, such as math, he feels more work is needed before these programs can be used for subjects like understanding history or analyzing poems. In fact, he cautions, computer programs may never be appropriate for this type of study.

The Importance of Hard Work

Hastings has been very successful in his life endeavors, but that success has required hard work and persistence. "Being an entrepreneur," he explains, "is about patience and persistence, not the quick buck, and everything great is hard and takes a long time."[79] He insists that there are no shortcuts to success. Hastings has put a great deal of patience and persistence into the things he wants, and his achievements in both education and the world of entertainment are proof that such hard work can pay off.

Chapter 5

Looking to the Future

No matter how successful he becomes, Hastings refuses to relax and simply enjoy that success. Instead, he continually looks to the future, taking notice of criticism and the possible ways he could fail, and coming up with innovative ideas to help him stay successful. Hastings says that he remains constantly inspired by the fear that he could fail at any time. This means that he actually welcomes negative comments because they help expose potential weaknesses. According to Hastings, "I think it is healthy to have smart people make a number of negative arguments about Netflix. It sharpens our thinking."[80] In fact, Hastings himself is the one who comes up with many of these negative arguments. He explains, "I see all the imperfections in Netflix. I see all the things that aren't working. At the office I'm the one that says 'we suck'. Don't get me wrong; we are better than everyone else, but we suck compared to what we are going to be."[81]

> "I think it is healthy to have smart people make a number of negative arguments about Netflix. It sharpens our thinking."[80]
>
> —Reed Hastings.

Although some of Hastings's innovative ideas have failed—for example, the Qwikster disaster—he has been very successful overall. After bringing Netflix back to success following its near failure in 2011, Hastings has focused on expanding the company worldwide, adding new content, and addressing all the other challenges that have arisen as streaming becomes more popular and he faces an increasing number of competitors.

Personal Life

Hastings lives in Santa Cruz, a beach community in central California, with his wife, Patty Quillin, and two teenage children. According to interviewers, he lives a laid-back lifestyle that does not resemble that of the typical billionaire. For example, in 2013 writer Nancy Hass wrote about visiting Hastings's home for an interview:

> Barely 1,800 square feet [162 sq. m.] and furnished with puffy couches and few personal touches beyond some family pictures on the mantel and four sleeping dogs his wife rescued from the shelter, it looks like the sort of pad a newly hired midlevel software executive might rent while he was looking for something to buy. Hastings's only domestic indulgence is a $5,000 handmade Italian espresso machine—"the closest I'm going to get to a Bentley," he jokes.[82]

In a 2014 article in the *New Yorker*, another writer reports that in addition to the four shelter dogs, Hastings also has four goats and ten chickens in his backyard.

Netflix Today

Netflix, the company he started in 1997, is expanding rapidly. By 2015 it had more than 50 million paid subscribers globally. MarketWatch reports that its net income in 2014 was $266.8 million. The company continues to offer both streaming and a DVD-by-mail service. The number of DVD-by-mail customers, however, is small compared to streaming customers and is steadily declining; meanwhile, streaming continues to increase in popularity. In 2012 Hastings said that he expected DVD subscribers to steadily decline forever. As a result, while Netflix still provides DVD rentals, it primarily focuses on streaming. Journalist Justin Fox points out that the company appears to pay very little attention to its DVD business. "Of the 2,500-odd words in the quarterly letter to shareholders [in January 2015]," Fox writes, "just 45 were devoted to plastic disks. In the 44-minute 'earnings interview' that followed, the DVD business didn't come up till the 41:33 mark."[83]

"TV in ten years is going to be one hundred per cent streamed."[84]

—Marc Andreessen, software engineer.

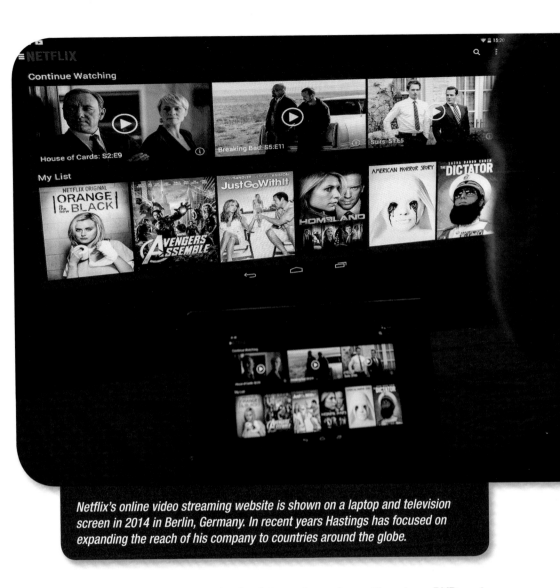

Netflix's online video streaming website is shown on a laptop and television screen in 2014 in Berlin, Germany. In recent years Hastings has focused on expanding the reach of his company to countries around the globe.

Hastings believes that in the future streaming will replace DVD rentals and traditional television service completely, and he intends that Netflix will be a major provider of that service. He is not the only one who believes in such a future. A large number of other companies, including Amazon and Hulu, are currently competing for streaming customers. Marc Andreessen, a software engineer who coinvented Mosaic, the first widely used Internet browser, insists, "TV in ten years is going to be one hundred per cent streamed. On demand. Internet Protocol. Based on computers and based on software."[84]

Eliminating Managed Dissatisfaction

Hastings argues that Netflix is far superior to the traditional model of entertainment provided by television networks and satellite companies, also referred to as multichannel video program distributors (MVPDs). These MVPDs usually force consumers to subscribe to a large group of channels, not just the ones they want, and often make them sign contracts and pay high subscription fees. In addition, movies and television shows on the various channels are scheduled at set times, and viewers need to wait until that time to watch a show or record it to view later. Furthermore, new television shows are typically released only one episode at a time, in many cases making viewers wait a week to view the next episode. Finally, many channels have regular breaks for commercials and promotional messages. Hastings argues that while consumers have been forced to endure this system for many years, most people do not like it. He calls the system managed dissatisfaction.

In contrast to the managed dissatisfaction that Hastings dislikes, Netflix is focused on giving consumers what they want, when they want it. It gives them the freedom to watch whatever show they want, whenever they want to watch it, and on whatever device they choose. In addition, there are no contracts and no commercials, and all episodes of a show are released at once. The Netflix website states, "We are a relief from the complexity and frustration that embody most MVPD relationships with their customers. . . . We are about the freedom of on-demand and the fun of indulgent viewing. We are about the flexibility of any screen any time."[85]

Binge Watching

Because Netflix makes every episode of a television show available at once, it has popularized something called binge watching. This means that rather than watching only one episode at a time, many viewers watch multiple episodes back to back. "Think of it as entertainment that's more like books," Hastings explains. "You get to control and watch, and you get to do all the chapters of a book at the same time, because you have all the episodes."[86] According to Ted Sarandos, chief content officer at Netflix, viewing data reveals that the majority of people who stream from Netflix would rather have the whole season of a show available at once so they can watch it at their own pace. A 2013 survey of 3,078 adults in the United States by Harris Interactive came to the same conclusion. It found that 79 percent of streamers believe that watching several episodes of their favorite show at once makes their viewing experience more enjoyable.

Original Programming

In addition to providing on-demand viewing, Netflix has become successful by creating original programming. It premiered its first original show, *Lilyhammer*, in 2011, releasing all episodes at once. *Lilyhammer* is about a fictional New York gangster trying to start a new life in Norway. The political drama *House of Cards* followed *Lilyhammer* and has won numerous Emmy Awards. Emmys recognize excellence in American

Giving to Charity

Hastings has been enormously successful financially, but he has also been enormously generous with his vast earnings. In 2012 Hastings and his wife made a major commitment to charitable giving when they signed the Giving Pledge. The Giving Pledge is a program whereby some of the world's wealthiest people have pledged to give more than half of their wealth to charitable causes or philanthropy, either during their lifetimes or in their wills. Individuals can choose which charities they would like to support. In their pledge letter, Hastings and his wife state, "It's an honor to be able to try to help our community, our country and our planet through our philanthropy. We are thrilled to join with other fortunate people to pledge a majority of our assets to be invested in others. We hope through this community that we can learn as we go, and do our best to make a positive difference for many."

Reed Hastings and Patty Quillin, "Current Pledgers," The Giving Pledge. http://givingpledge.org.

A NETFLIX ORIGINAL SERIES

|ORANGE|
is the new |BLACK|

EVERY SENTENCE IS A STORY

ALL EPISODES
JULY 11

ONLY ON
NETFLIX

Netflix has expanded its business to include original programming. Among its critically acclaimed series is Orange Is the New Black.

television programming. *House of Cards* was the first online-only show to receive an Emmy. Many other original shows have followed, including the popular *Orange Is the New Black*. Sarandos says Netflix will continue to offer new programming each year. In his opinion, "We can successfully support about 20 original scripted series every year, with a new series or a new season every two to three weeks."[87]

Content for Children

Netflix has also started to greatly expand its children's programming. In 2014 it was reported that only 3 percent of Netflix viewers were children. Thus, by attracting younger viewers, Netflix could increase its number of overall subscribers. Although children cannot sign up for their own subscriptions, they can influence their parents to do so. In 2013 Netflix announced a deal with the DreamWorks Animation studio that will bring about three hundred hours of original children's programming exclusively to Netflix. Some of the shows will be based on existing DreamWorks movies such as *Madagascar* and *Shrek*. In 2014 Netflix announced that it would be releasing a new version of *The Magic School Bus*, an animated show from the 1990s that remains popular today.

Utilizing Viewing Data

In addition to continually seeking out new content, Netflix focuses on providing content that viewers will like. One way it does this is by analyzing customer data. Whenever customers stream movies and television shows from Netflix, they are creating a digital record of their viewing habits. This record is surprisingly detailed. As journalist Andrew Leonard reports, "The company knows more about our viewing habits than many of us realize. Netflix doesn't know merely what we're watching, but when, where and with what kind of device we're watching. It keeps a record of every time we pause the action—or rewind, or fast-forward— and how many of us abandon a show entirely after watching for a few minutes."[88] Netflix analyzes this information to get a better understanding of what its customers like. It uses the results of this analysis to help it decide which type of programming to offer viewers in its effort to get the largest number of viewers possible. Sarandos says that Netflix is very calculating in what it buys. The company puts actors' names and the show types through the algorithms it has created to determine the likely size of an audience. He says, "I can justify the spend with our data and do so with a far greater degree of confidence

> "[Netflix] knows more about our viewing habits than many of us realize."[88]
>
> —Andrew Leonard, journalist.

than the television networks."[89] Netflix also uses its data when creating its original programming, for instance, using actors and themes that the majority of its customers seem to enjoy.

However, some people worry about the impact of all this data analysis. Leonard asks, "If Netflix perfects the job of giving us exactly what we want, when and how will we be exposed to things that are new and different, the movies and TV shows we would never imagine we might like unless given the chance?"[90] In fact, Leonard and others worry that new and different things might not even be created in the first place.

Continual Expansion

As well as focusing on expanding its content, Netflix continues to expand its service around the world. "It is no secret that we want Netflix to be a global product," says Sarandos. "That is the mission."[91] The company's first expansion was to Canada in 2010, where it offered an unlimited streaming plan for $7.99 a month. Latin America came next in 2011, followed by the United Kingdom and Nordic countries in 2012. In 2013 Netflix expanded to the Netherlands, and in 2014 it became available in the European countries of Germany, France, Luxembourg, Belgium, Austria, and Switzerland. By 2015 Netflix was available in more than forty countries.

> "The essence of net neutrality is that ISPs such as AT&T and Comcast don't restrict, influence or otherwise meddle with the choices consumers make."[92]
>
> —Reed Hastings.

Internet Neutrality

One recent threat to Netflix's expansion is disagreement over the issue of who should pay for the Internet service required to support streaming. Internet service providers (ISPs) say that Netflix drives the largest amount of streaming content during peak hours, and they insist that all this traffic is slowing streaming rates. They argue that Netflix should pay a fee to keep its data streaming smoothly. Hastings counters that this goes against the principle of Internet neutrality. Internet neutrality is the belief that Internet service should be provided equally to everyone, and ISPs should not be allowed to treat certain businesses

Turning Away from DVD Rentals

After the Qwikster failure, Hastings recognized that while he wanted Netflix to focus on streaming, the company needed to retain its DVD-by-mail service—too many of its customers demanded it. However, retaining the service did not mean he had to do anything to promote it. Instead, following the announcement that he would no longer be going ahead with Qwikster, Hastings stressed that although Netflix would continue to offer its DVD rental program, it would be focusing on streaming. He said, "Going forward we will be very aggressive on promoting streaming Netflix and the benefits, and anyone who wants to also subscribe to DVDs will be very welcome, but we are going to be pushing and promoting streaming." According to a 2012 news article, Hastings had no plans to market the DVD service or try to increase its subscribers. Instead, he explained that Netflix's "primary goal is to keep it stable, very high functioning" and "not to disturb it."

Quoted in William D. Cohan, "Seeing Red," *Vanity Fair*, February 2, 2012. www.vanityfair.com.

Reuters, "Netflix CEO Reed Hastings: 'We Expect DVD Subscribers to Decline Forever,'" January 25, 2012. www.reuters.com.

or individuals—such as Netflix—differently than others. Hastings explains, "The essence of net neutrality is that ISPs such as AT&T and Comcast don't restrict, influence or otherwise meddle with the choices consumers make."[92]

The argument over Internet neutrality is not limited to Hastings and ISPs. This issue has also provoked intense debate within the US government. President Barack Obama is strongly in favor of Internet neutrality, insisting that such freedom helps promote competition and preserve democracy. He maintains,

An open Internet is essential to the American economy, and increasingly to our very way of life. By lowering the cost of launching a new idea, igniting new political movements, and bringing communities closer together, it has been one of the most significant democratizing influences the world has ever known. . . . We cannot allow Internet service providers (ISPs) to restrict the best access or to pick winners and losers in the online marketplace for services and ideas.[93]

In 2015 the FCC approved Internet neutrality rules which will require ISPs to treat all customers equally rather than providing different types of service—with different costs—to different types of customers. However most experts believe these rules will be challenged in court. As a result, debate over this issue is likely to continue in the future.

Reed Hastings demonstrates how various gaming devices can be used to stream content during a 2010 news conference marking Netflix's expansion into Canada. The company has since moved into Latin America, the United Kingdom, and Europe.

HBO

In addition to the possibility of paying tolls to ISPs, Netflix faces the threat of many competitors who provide similar services. One of the biggest is HBO, a television network that is available through various satellite and cable television companies. HBO has its own original programming, including the extremely popular shows *Game of Thrones* and *True Blood*. In 2013 Netflix surpassed HBO in total domestic subscribers. However, HBO has many more subscribers worldwide than Netflix, about 117 million in 2013, compared with Netflix at more than 40 million. A recent announcement by HBO indicates that the competition between Netflix and HBO is likely to get even fiercer in the future. HBO announced that it will launch a video streaming service in 2015. In the past HBO has been sold as part of a satellite or cable subscription package, making it a slightly different market from Netflix. Thus, its decision to offer its content online like Netflix is likely to result in greater competition between the two companies.

Continued Activism in Education

As well as striving to expand Netflix and keep ahead of competitors, Hastings continues to work to improve education in the United States. In 2014 he generated a lot of publicity by publicly criticizing school boards. School boards are legislative bodies elected by the citizens of that district. They play an important role in determining school policy. However, Hastings argues that because school boards are established by public election, their leadership and goals are constantly changing; as a result, nothing effective is accomplished. He argues that a privately established group of leaders—such as those at charter schools—is more effective. He maintains, "[Charter schools] constantly get better every year . . . because they have stable governance—they don't have an elected school board."[94] Many people were outraged by Hastings's comments, insisting that school boards are a vital part of democracy. Matt Haney, a member of the San Francisco Unified School District board, believes school boards preserve democracy. "When a perspective is missing from the board, a community can elect someone to represent it. When the curriculum, budget or policies don't reflect the values or priorities of a community, such as discipline policies that push out black and Latino students, the people can change that." Haney insists, "Without elected school boards, there is no accountability to the community."[95]

The Value of Being Unique

Although Hastings's comments about school boards were not well received by many people, they do reflect the fact that he often has a unique perspective and is not afraid to voice it and act on it. This is part of what has made him so successful. Marc Randolph, the cofounder of Netflix, says that early on he realized that Hastings was going to do something big. He insists that from the beginning he looked at Hastings and thought, "This guy has unbelievable capacity, and range of curiosity, and ways to create ideas and assimilate them in different ways."[96] Hastings's unique ideas, combined with his hard work and persistence, pushed him into the ranks of billionaire in 2014. Reaching billionaire status does not mean Hastings is resting easy, and it has not silenced his critics, but Hastings seems to like a continuing challenge. Back in 2005 he commented, "We've always struggled, but in the end I think that's given us character." He remarked that the struggle has simply made him enjoy his success that much more. "To be doubted and be successful is particularly satisfying."[97]

Source Notes

Introduction: Changing How People Access Entertainment

1. John A. Byrne, *World Changers: 25 Entrepreneurs Who Changed Business as We Knew It.* New York: Penguin, 2011, p. 39.
2. Quoted in Julia Boorstin, "CNBC Exclusive: CNBC Transcript: Netflix CEO Reed Hastings Speaks with CNBC's Julia Boorstin," CNBC, October 16, 2014. www.cnbc.com.
3. Netflix, "Netflix Long Term View," October 15, 2014. http://ir.netflix .com.
4. Quoted in Ken Auletta, "Outside the Box: Netflix and the Future of Television," *New Yorker*, February 3, 2014. www.newyorker.com.
5. Larry Magid, "Magid: Lots of Younger People Abandoning Broadcast, Cable or Satellite TV," *San Jose Mercury News*, March 15, 2013. www .mercurynews.com.

Chapter One: Early Life

6. Reed Hastings, as told to Amy Zipkin, "Out of Africa, onto the Web," *New York Times*, December 17, 2006. www.nytimes.com.
7. Quoted in Emma Peters, "Live Stream: Netflix CEO Reed Hastings '83," *Bowdoin Orient*, October 4, 2013. http://bowdoinorient.com.
8. Quoted in Peters, "Live Stream."
9. Quoted in Peters, "Live Stream."
10. Quoted in Peters, "Live Stream."
11. Gina Keating, *Netflixed: The Epic Battle for America's Eyeballs.* New York: Penguin, 2012, p. 13.
12. Quoted in Margaret Warner, "Conversation: Tuxedo Park," *PBS Newshour*, July 22, 2002. www.pbs.org.
13. Hastings, "Out of Africa, onto the Web."
14. Quoted in Joanne Jacobs, "Disrupting the Education Monopoly," EducationNext, Winter 2005. http://educationnext org.
15. Hastings, "Out of Africa, onto the Web."

16. Quoted in Peters, "Live Stream."

17. Peters, "Live Stream."

18. Quoted in Byrne, *World Changers*, p. 38.

19. Quoted in Auletta, "Outside the Box."

20. Hastings, "Out of Africa, onto the Web."

21. Quoted in Jim Hopkins, "'Charismatic' Founder Keeps Netflix Adapting," *USA Today*, April 24, 2006. http://usatoday30.usatoday.com.

22. Quoted in Boris Veldhuijzen van Zanten, "Inspiring Entrepreneurs: What Netflix CEO Reed Hastings Has Learned in His Business Career," The Next Web, September 12, 2013. http://thenextweb.com.

23. Hastings, "Out of Africa, onto the Web."

24. Michelle Conlin, "Netflix: Flex to the Max," *Bloomberg Businessweek*, September 23, 2007. www.businessweek.com.

25. Quoted in Michael V. Copeland, "Reed Hastings: Leader of the Pack," *Fortune*, November 18, 2010. http://fortune.com.

Chapter Two: The Creation of Netflix

26. Quoted in Byrne, *World Changers*, p. 40.

27. Marc Randolph, "Netflix's First CEO on Reed Hastings and How the Company Really Got Started: Executive of the Year 2013," *Silicon Valley Business Journal*, January 9, 2014. www.bizjournals.com.

28. Marc Randolph, "Profile," LinkedIn. www.linkedin.com.

29. Marc Randolph, "It Isn't Lying If You Believe It," *Fortune*, May 13, 2011. http://fortune.com.

30. Quoted in Christopher Null, "How Netflix Is Fixing Hollywood by Finding a Market for Niche Titles—and Keeping Discs in Constant Circulation—the Online DVD Rental Pioneer Is Shaking Up the Movie Biz," CNN, July 1, 2003. http://money.cnn.com.

31. Quoted in Gary Rivlin, "Does the Kid Stay in the Picture?," *New York Times*, February 22, 2005. www.nytimes.com.

32. Randolph, "Netflix's First CEO on Reed Hastings and How the Company Really Got Started."

33. Quoted in Glenn Lovell, "From the Archive, 1998: Netflix Supplies Obscure DVD Flicks," *San Jose Mercury News*, July 10, 1998. www.mercurynews.com.

34. Reed Hastings, as told to Patrick J. Sauer, "How I Did It: Reed Hastings, Netflix," *Inc.*, December 1, 2005. www.inc.com.

35. Copeland, "Reed Hastings."

36. Quoted in Clive Thompson, "If You Liked This, You're Sure to Love That," *New York Times*, November 24, 2008. www.nytimes.com.

37. Hastings, "How I Did It."

38. Jacobs, "Disrupting the Education Monopoly."

Chapter Three: Success at Netflix

39. Quoted in Tim Arango, "Time Warner Views Netflix as a Fading Star," *New York Times*, December 12, 2010. www.nytimes.com.

40. Quoted in Auletta, "Outside the Box."

41. Quoted in James Ledbetter, "America's Most Underestimated Company," *Slate*, September 1, 2010. www.slate.com.

42. Hastings, "How I Did It."

43. Quoted in Alyssa Abkowitz, "How Netflix Got Started," *Fortune*, January 28, 2009. http://archive.fortune.com.

44. Quoted in Rivlin, "Does the Kid Stay in the Picture?"

45. David Pogue, "In the Competition for DVD Rentals by Mail, Two Empires Strike Back," *New York Times*, March 31, 2005. www.nytimes .com.

46. Quoted in Marc Graser, "Epic Fail: How Blockbuster Could Have Owned Netflix," *Variety*, November 12, 2013. http://variety.com.

47. Rick Newman, "How Netflix (and Blockbuster) Killed Blockbuster," *U.S. News & World Report*, September 23, 2010. http://money.us news.com.

48. Quoted in Newman, "How Netflix (and Blockbuster) Killed Blockbuster."

49. Quoted in Ledbetter, "America's Most Underestimated Company."

50. Hastings, "How I Did It."

51. Randolph, "Netflix's First CEO on Reed Hastings and How the Company Really Got Started."

52. Pogue, "In the Competition for DVD Rentals by Mail."

53. Netflix, "DVD Terms and Conditions," June 6, 2014. www.netflix.com.

54. Quoted in Eliot Van Buskirk, "How the Netflix Prize Was Won," *Wired*, September 22, 2009. www.wired.com.

55. Quoted in Rivlin, "Does the Kid Stay in the Picture?"

56. Quoted in Henry Blodget and Dan Frommer, "Exclusive Interview with Netflix CEO Reed Hastings: Netflix's Market Opportunity Is a Lot Bigger than You Think," *Business Insider*, April 4, 2011. www.business insider.com.

57. Copeland, "Reed Hastings."

58. Netflix, "Q4 10 Letter to Shareholders and Financial Results," January 26, 2011. http://ir.netflix.com.

Chapter Four: Persevering to Reach His Goals

59. Reed Hastings, "An Explanation and Some Reflections," *Netflix* (blog), September 18, 2011. http://blog.netflix.com.

60. Jessie Becker, "Netflix Introduces New Plans and Announces Price Changes," *Netflix* (blog), July 12, 2011. http://blog.netflix.com.

61. Jacqui North, comment to Becker, "Netflix Introduces New Plans and Announces Price Changes."

62. Anonymous, comment to Becker, "Netflix Introduces New Plans and Announces Price Changes."

63. Anonymous, comment to Becker, "Netflix Introduces New Plans and Announces Price Changes."

64. Hastings, "An Explanation and Some Reflections."

65. Quoted in Stu Woo, "Under Fire, Netflix Rewinds DVD Plan," *Wall Street Journal*, October 11, 2011. www.wsj.com.

66. Quoted in Woo, "Under Fire, Netflix Rewinds DVD Plan."

67. Quoted in William D. Cohan, "Seeing Red," *Vanity Fair*, February 2, 2012. www.vanityfair.com.

68. Quoted in Veldhuijzen van Zanten, "Inspiring Entrepreneurs."

69. Patty McCord, "How Netflix Reinvented HR," *Harvard Business Review*, January 2014. https://hbr.org.

70. Quoted in Bill Snyder, "Netflix Founder Reed Hastings: Make as Few Decisions as Possible," Graduate School of Stanford Business, November 3, 2014. www.gsb.stanford.edu.

71. Quoted in Michael Gillis, "Head in the Cloud," *Cornell Engineering Magazine*, Fall 2011. www.engineering.cornell.edu.

72. Quoted in Robert J. Grossman, "Tough Love at Netflix," *HR Magazine*, April 1, 2010. www.shrm.org.

73. McCord, "How Netflix Reinvented HR."

74. John Patrick Pullen, "How These 24 Business Leaders Stay Productive and Successful: Reed Hastings, Co-founder and CEO of Netflix," *Time*, January 6, 2014. http://time100.time.com.

75. Quoted in Jason Riley, "Movie Man," *Wall Street Journal*, February 9, 2008. http://online.wsj.com.

76. Michael Kirst, quoted in Joan O'C. Hamilton, "Home Movies," *Stanford Alumni Magazine*, January/February 2006. https://alumni.stanford.edu.

77. Quoted in Riley, "Movie Man."

78. Quoted in Hamilton, "Home Movies."

79. Quoted in Byrne, *World Changers*, p. 39.

Chapter Five: Looking to the Future

80. Quoted in Copeland, "Reed Hastings."

81. Quoted in Veldhuijzen van Zanten, "Inspiring Entrepreneurs."

82. Nancy Hass, "And the Award for the Next HBO Goes to . . . ," *GQ*, February 2013. www.gq.com.

83. Justin Fox, "Netflix and DVDs, Still Together," *Bloomberg View*, January 21, 2015. www.bloombergview.com.

84. Quoted in Auletta, "Outside the Box."

85. Netflix, "Netflix Long Term View."

86. Quoted in Auletta, "Outside the Box."

87. Quoted in Gary Levin, "Netflix Has Big Plans for 2015 Originals," *USA Today*, January 8, 2015. www.usatoday.com.

88. Andrew Leonard, "How Netflix Is Turning Viewers into Puppets," *Salon*, February 1, 2013. www.salon.com.

89. Quoted in Ashlee Vance, "Netflix, Reed Hastings Survive Missteps to Join Silicon Valley's Elite," *Bloomberg Businessweek*, May 9, 2013. www.businessweek.com.

90. Leonard, "How Netflix Is Turning Viewers into Puppets."

91. Quoted in Emily Steel, "How to Build an Empire, the Netflix Way," *New York Times*, November 29, 2014. www.nytimes.com.

92. Reed Hastings, "Internet Tolls and the Case for Strong Net Neutrality," *Netflix* (blog), March 20, 2014. http://blog.netflix.com.

93. Barack Obama, "Net Neutrality: President Obama's Plan for a Free and Open Internet: The President's Statement," White House. www .whitehouse.gov.

94. Quoted in Valerie Strauss, "Netflix's Reed Hastings Has a Big Idea: Kill Elected School Boards (Update)," *Washington Post*, March 14, 2014. www.washingtonpost.com.

95. Matt Haney, "Reed Hastings Is Wrong: A School Board Member's Defense," *San Jose Mercury News*, March 14, 2014. www.mercury news.com.

96. Randolph, "Netflix's First CEO on Reed Hastings and How the Company Really Got Started."

97. Quoted in Rivlin, "Does the Kid Stay in the Picture?"

Important Events in the Life of Reed Hastings

1960

Wilmot Reed Hastings Jr. is born in Boston, Massachusetts.

1983

After graduating from Bowdoin College, Hastings joins the Peace Corps, traveling to Africa as a math teacher.

1988

Hastings graduates from Stanford University in California with a master's degree in artificial intelligence.

1991

Hastings founds his own company, Pure Software.

1997

Netflix is founded by Hastings and Marc Randolph.

1998

Hastings is part of a campaign that successfully forces California to change its restrictive charter school law.

2000

Governor Gray Davis appoints Hastings to the California State Board of Education, where he serves until 2004.

2002

Netflix becomes a public company.

2006

The Netflix Prize is announced; $1 million will be awarded to the person or team that can improve the Netflix recommendation system by 10 percent.

2007

Netflix launches its streaming service.

2010

Fortune magazine names Hastings Businessperson of the Year.

2011

Hundreds of thousands of subscribers leave Netflix after Hastings announces a price increase and a split between the DVD-by-mail and streaming services.

2012

Netflix debuts its first original show, *Lilyhammer*.

2013

Netflix's original show *House of Cards* becomes the first online-only show to win an Emmy Award.

2014

Netflix expands service to Austria, Belgium, France, Germany, Luxembourg, and Switzerland; it reaches a global membership of more than 50 million.

For Further Research

Books

John A. Byrne, *World Changers: 25 Entrepreneurs Who Changed Business as We Knew It*. New York: Penguin, 2011.

Gina Keating, *Netflixed: The Epic Battle for America's Eyeballs*. New York: Penguin, 2012.

Internet Sources

Alyssa Abkowitz, "How Netflix Got Started," *Fortune*, January 28, 2009. http://archive.fortune.com/2009/01/27/news/newsmakers/hastings _netflix.fortune/index.htm.

Ken Auletta, "Outside the Box: Netflix and the Future of Television," *New Yorker*, February 3, 2014. www.newyorker.com/magazine/2014/02/03 /outside-the-box-2.

Michael V. Copeland, "Reed Hastings: Leader of the Pack," *Fortune*, November 18, 2010. http://fortune.com/2010/11/18/reed-hastings-leader -of-the-pack.

Nancy Hass, "And the Award for the Next HBO Goes to . . . ," *GQ*, February 2013. www.gq.com/entertainment/movies-and-tv/201302/netflix-found er-reed-hastings-house-of-cards-arrested-development?printable=true.

Reed Hastings, "Internet Tolls and the Case for Strong Net Neutrality," *Netflix* (blog), March 20, 2014. http://blog.netflix.com/2014/03/internet -tolls-and-case-for-strong-net.htm.

Reed Hastings, as told to Patrick J. Sauer, "How I Did It: Reed Hastings, Netflix," *Inc.*, December 1, 2005. www.inc.com/magazine/20061201/qa -hastings.html.

Reed Hastings, as told to Amy Zipkin, "Out of Africa, onto the Web," *New York Times*, December 17, 2006. www.nytimes.com/2006/12/17/jobs/17boss.html?pagewanted=print&_r=0.

Andrew Leonard, "How Netflix Is Turning Viewers into Puppets," *Salon*, February 1, 2013. www.salon.com/2013/02/01/how_netflix_is_turning_viewers_into_puppets.

Patty McCord, "How Netflix Reinvented HR," *Harvard Business Review*, January 2014. https://hbr.org/2014/01/how-netflix-reinvented-hr.

Marc Randolph, "Netflix's First CEO on Reed Hastings and How the Company Really Got Started," *Silicon Valley Business Journal*, January 9, 2014. www.bizjournals.com/sanjose/news/2014/01/08/netflixs-first-ceo-on-reed-hastings.html?page=all.

Index

Picture Credits

Cover: © Jack Dempsey/AP/Corbis

Associated Press: 20, 25, 28, 44

© Lacy Atkins/San Francisco Chronicle/Corbis: 39

© Bettmann/Corbis: 11

© Mike Cassese/Reuters/Corbis: 62

Pippa Hetherington/Earthstock/Newscom: 15

© Bernd von Jutrczenka/dpa/Corbis: 55

Netflix/Photofest: 58

Dick Schmidt/SUMA Press/Newscom: 31

Michael Tercha/MCT/Newscom: 35, 48

© Kimberly White/Corbis: 8

About the Author

Andrea C. Nakaya, a native of New Zealand, holds a BA in English and an MA in communications from San Diego State University. She has written and edited more than thirty-five books on current issues. She currently lives in Encinitas, California, with her husband and their two children, Natalie and Shane.